TRANSFORMED

UNTIL CHRIST IS FORMED IN ME

30 Day Devotional

Nate Stevens

Unless otherwise indicated, Scripture taken from the New King James Version. Copyright © 1982 by Thomas Nelson, Inc. Used by permission. All rights reserved.

Scripture quotations marked (NIV) are taken from the Holy Bible, NEW INTERNATIONAL VERSION®, NIV® Copyright © 1973, 1978, 1984, 2011 by Biblica, Inc.® Used by permission. All rights reserved worldwide.

Scripture quotations marked (NLT) are taken from the Holy Bible, New Living Translation, copyright ©1996, 2004, 2015 by Tyndale House Foundation. Used by permission of Tyndale House Publishers, a Division of Tyndale House Ministries, Carol Stream, Illinois 60188. All rights reserved.

Scripture quotations marked (KJV) are taken from the Holy Bible, King James Version. Rights in the Authorized Version in the United Kingdom are vested in the Crown. Reproduced by permission of the Crown's patentee, Cambridge University Press.

First Edition, 2020
ISBN 10: 978-1-64590-011-5

Published by Kingdom Winds Publishing.
6 Charleston Oak Lane, Greenville, SC 29615
www.kingdomwinds.com
publishing@kingdomwinds.com
Printed in the United States of America.

Cover Design by Christine Dupre

The views expressed in this book are not necessarily those of the publisher.

ACKNOWLEDGMENT

First and foremost, thank you, Jesus Christ, my Lord and Savior, for allowing me the privilege of joining You on such a transformational journey. Not only do You love me as You found me, but You also love me enough to continue transforming me into who You created and called me to be! Hallelujah!

Additionally, thank you, Karen Stevens, for seemingly endless hours watching me study, research, and write, then helping choose which devotions to include as well as develop the cover concept. Along with my heart, you have my thanks and appreciation. I love you!

Finally, thank you, Gary and Elizabeth Suess and the Kingdom Winds family for your partnership in this endeavor. I am grateful for your vision and ministry to support authors, songwriters, artists, and others as they fulfill their roles in building and equipping the eternal Kingdom of God. Bless you!

ENDORSEMENTS

The anointing on Nate's life is such a gift to the body of Christ. His heart for God and passion for God is so infectious and inspiring. When he speaks or writes, the Lord uses him to equip the saints for the work of the ministry that we are all called to do with sharper swords and greater passion. He and Karen have been such wonderful blessings to Covenant Fellowship Church. I know this devotional will be used by the Lord to transform lives into more of what God intended for them to be.

Michael Booker, Lead Pastor

Covenant Fellowship Church—Bristol, VA

Nate Stevens is a gifted communicator—an excellent student and teacher of Scripture. Whether at a conference, a Bible study he's leading, a one-on-one conversation, or through something he's written, I always appreciate what he has to say. This devotional is no exception. It is pithy and powerful. Transformation is the journey (and the destination) for every child of God. Thanks, Nate, for helping us along the way—and for reminding us that His Word and prayer are the way. These devotions aren't long, but they're life-changing. Now, for the next 30 days and until That Day, "Change my heart, oh God."

Greg Baker, Executive Pastor

Central Church—Charlotte, NC

INTRODUCTION

God invests Himself in and through us while gradually, lovingly molding us into His likeness! As a matter of fact, He created, called, and purposed us for such a transformation!

The lifelong journey of becoming Christlike involves a threefold process. First, it requires a supernatural, spiritual "new birth," followed by daily surrender to God's Word and His Spirit's influence. Second, it involves a determined rejection of conformity to the world, coupled with a passionate pursuit of holiness. Lastly, transformation into Christlikeness is predicated on a willingness to renew, even change, individual mindsets about anything not fully aligning with God's Word.

These concise daily devotions encourage such a powerful, transforming impact. May they be catalysts of change resonating within you throughout each day. More than just reading them daily, I encourage you to meditate on them—applying them to life and allowing them to ignite a deeper, more intimate walk with God.

Above all else, may this 30-day journey begin a personal transformation "until Christ is formed in you" (Galatians 4:19).

Nate Stevens

෪ᠫᡄᡓ

TRANSFORMATIONAL JOURNEY – DAY 1

Ready and Willing for God's Transformation
(Romans 12:2)

"Be transformed by the renewing of your mind." God's transformation seldom appears or arrives as we expect it. Sometimes we seek God through the lenses of human experience and perspective, failing to understand our rationale is severely restricted. We long to meet Him in the peaceful meadow, but He develops reliance on Him through rough terrain. We desire to walk the straight and narrow path, yet complain when navigating His turbulent storms. We ask Him to transform us into His likeness, then grumble when in His refining fire. We anxiously await some new spiritual revelation, but overlook His Word already given. Oh, we claim to be willing to die for Him, but are we willing to live for Him?

Loving Father, renew my mind to enable Your transformation.

TRANSFORMATIONAL JOURNAL – DAY 1

What personal mindset needs God's transforming renewal?

_____

_____

_____

_____

_____

_____

_____

_____

_____

_____

ഇ⊃⊂ഓ

TRANSFORMATIONAL JOURNEY – DAY 2

Allowing God to Capture Our Hearts
(Ezekiel 14:4-5, NLT)

"I, the Lord...do this to capture the minds and hearts of all my people." God often distresses our passions and desires (whether good or bad) because He seeks to capture or seize our hearts and minds. Only God's internal change affects habitual, demonstrated behavior. Instead of focusing on external behaviors, God captures and changes hearts. Aside from forcibly removing money-changers from the Temple, even Jesus refrained from legislated morality. When He has the heart, He has the person including mindset, behaviors, desires, character, and choices. Unfortunately, quite often we have "idols" (people, possessions, places, careers) that we treasure more than God. So, He pursues us relentlessly until we willingly surrender everything to Him and allow Him to wholly capture us.

Capture me today, loving Father.

TRANSFORMATIONAL JOURNAL – DAY 2

What can I release today so God can capture my whole heart?

_____

_____

_____

_____

_____

_____

_____

_____

_____

_____

෩෩෩

TRANSFORMATIONAL JOURNEY – DAY 3

God Transforms When There Is a Willingness to Change
(Luke 15:17)

God does not coerce or force Himself upon anyone. Until a person willingly and humbly accepts God's change, he continues life blindly unaware of eternally relevant matters. Unless a person's spirit is "reborn from above" (John 3:3-6), he remains spiritually flat-lining in sin. Even when a believer strays from God into the "far country" of sin (Luke 15:13), he experiences a soul-searching event borne out of hardship and heartache until he eventually "comes to his senses" and decides whether or not the pigpen of self will be his destiny. Until such time as repentance begins the journey toward transformation, he is doomed by his own choice to continue eating the bland, unhealthy husks intended for pigs.

Father, I repent, surrender to You, and willingly
accept Your transforming work in me.

TRANSFORMATIONAL JOURNAL– DAY 3

What habit or area of my life needs repentance and surrender to God?

_____

_____

_____

_____

_____

_____

_____

_____

_____

_____

_____

TRANSFORMATIONAL JOURNEY – DAY 4

God Calls Us Out of Our Caves (1 Kings 19:9-18)

When life becomes too frightening, disorderly, or overwhelming, we tend to hide in caves of disappointment, despair, discouragement, or depression. In our self-made prisons of perceived comfort and safety, we forget they are still dark, damp, lonely places. They do not comfort, nor do they help us face whatever lies ahead. They merely create illusions of safety. However, God calls us out—He does not abandon us in the loneliness and doubt of the caves. He does not arrive in gusts of wind, shattering earthquakes, or blazing fires. Those are simply demonstrations of His power. No, His intimate whispers penetrate the fog of our minds, compelling us to stand before Him, renewed in strength and recommissioned in service.

Father, release me from my current cave.

TRANSFORMATIONAL JOURNAL – DAY 4

What current "cave" is restricting me from God's purpose?

_____

_____

_____

_____

_____

_____

_____

_____

_____

_____

TRANSFORMATIONAL JOURNEY – DAY 5

A Change of Mind (Ephesians 4:17-24)

"You should no longer walk as...the Gentiles walk, in the futility of their mind." Followers of Christ are called to a new mindset. "Be renewed in the spirit of your mind" (Ephesians 4:23). After spiritual rebirth in Christ, we no longer pursue the futile, empty, ignorant thoughts and desires of the world. Contrarily, we put on the new man and reflect the renewed mindset of God's righteousness and holiness. No longer alienated from God or blind of heart, we passionately pursue the "measure of the stature of the fullness of Christ" (Ephesians 4:13). The deceitful cravings of the old man are not fulfilling; the fullness of Christ is the purpose for which we were created.

Father, this realization motivates me to "walk worthy" of Your calling (Ephesians 4:1).

TRANSFORMATIONAL JOURNAL - DAY 5

How is God transforming (renewing) my mind?

_____

_____

_____

_____

_____

_____

_____

_____

_____

_____

෨෧෬

TRANSFORMATIONAL JOURNEY – DAY 6

God Often Removes Specific Strengths to Motivate Complete Reliance on Him (Amos 2:14-16)

"The strong shall not strengthen his power, nor shall the mighty deliver himself." Whether it is wealth, physical strength, business acumen, intelligence, or even a soft heart, what we value more than God, He consistently and persistently removes or breaks until our all-compelling desire is Him alone. He slows the fast, weakens the strong, humbles the proud, deprives the rich, condemns the self-righteous, and judges the unrepentant. Until He is the sole source of a person's confidence, security, faith, and reliance for everything—yes, even eternity—His work remains incomplete. His loving and relentless goal is radical transformation until "Christ is formed in you" (Galatians 4:19).

Father, help me surrender even my strengths if they jeopardize complete reliance on You.

TRANSFORMATIONAL JOURNAL – DAY 6

What strength may be preventing my complete reliance on God?

_____

_____

_____

_____

_____

_____

_____

_____

_____

TRANSFORMATIONAL JOURNEY – DAY 7

Intentional Thinking Patterns (Colossians 3:1-3)

"Seek those things which are above...set your mind on things above, not on things on the earth." There is an earnest intentionality in the pursuit of Godly things. We deliberately seek Him, His Word, and His ways. We purposefully create mental dispositions that align with the mind of Christ (Philippians 2:5). We do this by habitually shedding the old, dead self (Ephesians 4:22) and walking in Christ's newness of abundant life (Romans 6:4). In deliberately realigning our focus and priorities, our perspectives change from the temporary to the eternal. Though the earthly walk is an intentional struggle, one day, the former things will pass away with all things made new (Revelation 21:4-5).

Heavenly Father, until Your kingdom comes, help me daily align my mind with Yours.

TRANSFORMATIONAL JOURNAL – DAY 7

How will I align my pattern of thinking to a heavenly mindset?

_____

_____

_____

_____

_____

_____

_____

_____

_____

છે)(૯૪

TRANSFORMATIONAL JOURNEY – DAY 8

Distinguish Between the Holy and the Unholy
(Ezekiel 22:26)

"Her priests have violated My law and profaned My holy things; they have not distinguished between the holy and unholy." Discerning between murdering someone and attending church is usually easy. However, complexity arises when moral and ethical lines blur due to cultural pressure, uncontrolled personal desires, or conformity with the world. Thankfully, God's standard remains unchanged—His Word abides forever. With constancy comes reliability. He cannot change, modify, or alter His character. He remains the same yesterday, today, and forever. It is we who must change to align with His moral code.

Heavenly Father, help me embrace Your righteous standard immediately and fully. When making choices, guide me to discern the holy, then empower me to firmly align myself with Your holy standard.

TRANSFORMATIONAL JOURNAL – DAY 8

What subtle yet unholy habit is restricting God's transformation?

_____

_____

_____

_____

_____

_____

_____

_____

_____

᯾ᴑᴑᴂ

TRANSFORMATIONAL JOURNEY – DAY 9

A Deliberate Change of Mind (Philippians 2:5)

"Let this mind be in you which was also in Christ Jesus." Letting something happen involves exercising individual allowance or choice. The mindset of Christ is not a mystical occurrence that happens against our will. It is a personal, ongoing, deliberate decision to be mentally disposed—an intentional change of mind— to place our affections on Jesus and adopt His mindset. Through the power of the Holy Spirit, we restrain all personal longings, all worldly cravings, and align our affections with heavenly desires (Colossians 3:10). We daily die to ourselves, take up His cross, and follow Him (Luke 9:23). We reckon ourselves dead to the world's deceptive distractions (Galatians 6:14) and alive to Christ's heart.

Holy Father, please transform my mindset to mirror Your own.

TRANSFORMATIONAL JOURNAL – DAY 9

How will I intentionally exchange my ingrained mindset for the mind of Christ?

_____

_____

_____

_____

_____

_____

_____

_____

_____

ℰͻℭℛ

TRANSFORMATIONAL JOURNEY – DAY 10

Unexpected Blessings in Unexpected Places
(Isaiah 43:20, NIV)

God said, "I provide water in the wilderness and streams in the wasteland, to give drink to my people." Notice it does not say He provides water beside a shaded oasis or in a blossoming meadow. That refreshing scenario would be what most of us expect. However, water in a dry, desolate desert is something only He can provide. At times, life can be a wilderness, a withering wasteland. In those barren seasons, when hearts, souls, and minds wilt under the scorching heat of adversity, there is only one true source of renewal. We flourish only when drinking deeply from God's Water of Life. Drinking daily from His Water revives, restores, and re-energizes, all while preventing spiritual heatstroke, fainting, and weariness on the journey.

Father God, make me thirsty for Your Word!

TRANSFORMATIONAL JOURNAL – DAY 10

*How will I incorporate quality "quiet time" with God
into my daily routine?*

_____

_____

_____

_____

_____

_____

_____

_____

_____

_____

TRANSFORMATIONAL JOURNEY – DAY 11

Holiness Characterizes God's Authentic People
(1 Peter 1:15)

"As He who called you is holy, you also be holy in all your conduct." People who truly desire to be "on fire" for God are characterized by His holiness and His righteousness—not personal standards, what they think is holy, or even the world's evolving standard of what is acceptable, right, moral, or culturally allowable. As living before Holy God, lives and lifestyles must be purified. The individual choice to walk in His righteousness ignites His fire of holiness. To walk in God's righteousness requires us to be rightly related to and aligned with Him, which brings us full circle to relationships. First, the relationship, then the fellowship, all leading to deeper intimacy with Him.

Heavenly Father, purify me in Your transforming fire
of holiness.

TRANSFORMATIONAL JOURNAL – DAY 11

What cultural influence or personal preference prevents my deeper intimacy with God?

_____

_____

_____

_____

_____

_____

_____

_____

_____

_____

TRANSFORMATIONAL JOURNEY – DAY 12

Are You Struggling Through Adversity Today?
(Ecclesiastes 7:14)

"In the day of prosperity be joyful, but in the day of adversity consider: surely God has appointed the one as well as the other." Dark caves, burning deserts, or fierce storms—all are places of isolated stress intended to transform us and strengthen our intimacy with Jesus. They each may represent seasons of overwhelming doubts, fears, and uncertainty. However, the longer we focus on the cave's darkness, the desert's heat, or the storm's fury, the less we focus on Him. This may explain why He sometimes leaves us in harsh circumstances. He desires our full attention, surrender, and commitment. But rest assured, He orchestrates every detail.

Loving Father, when adversity threatens, help me trust You with my cares and concerns (1 Peter 5:7).

TRANSFORMATIONAL JOURNAL – DAY 12

How is my current adversity pressing me closer to God?

_____

_____

_____

_____

_____

_____

_____

_____

_____

_____

TRANSFORMATIONAL JOURNEY – DAY 13

The Character of the New Man (Colossians 3:12-17)

"As the elect of God, holy and beloved, put on..." The implication of "put on" is to clothe oneself in a garment. This willful, intentional act involves an acceptance and incorporation of Godly traits and knowledge. We clothe ourselves with such characteristics as compassion, kindness, humility, meekness, patience, support, forgiveness, and love. But there also remains the "let the peace of God rule" where we deliberately allow His peace to reign in our hearts and His Word to permeate all aspects of our lives. With hearts, minds, souls, and bodies consumed with God's essence and influence, everything we do is for God's glory and purpose.

Loving Father, with the Holy Spirit working supernaturally within, I am empowered to put on and allow as You influence—both of which transform me into Your newness.

TRANSFORMATIONAL JOURNAL – DAY 13

What am I "putting on" today in my pursuit of God's holiness?

_____

_____

_____

_____

_____

_____

_____

_____

_____

❧❦

TRANSFORMATIONAL JOURNEY – DAY 14

God's Water Cleanses; His Fire Refines
(Numbers 31:23)

"Everything that can endure fire...put through the fire, and it shall be clean... But all that cannot endure fire...put through water." When surrendering our sins to God, He forgives and then purifies with the water of His Word and the power of the Holy Spirit. But when we stubbornly hold onto sinful lifestyles or selfish desires, deeper purification becomes necessary— God's refining fire. He lovingly disciplines through sovereignly orchestrated events or the natural consequences of our willful, unrepentant actions. God's consistent goal is to transform us into the image of His Son, Jesus Christ. He seeks to purify, never to consume.

Oh, God, please have Your perfect way in and through me. Cleanse and refine as You deem necessary. Help me surrender to Your water and avoid Your fire.

TRANSFORMATIONAL JOURNAL – DAY 14

How is God purifying me today?

_____

_____

_____

_____

_____

_____

_____

_____

_____

TRANSFORMATIONAL JOURNEY – DAY 15

The Stigma of a Christian (Galatians 6:17)

"I bear in my body the marks of the Lord Jesus." Carrying the cross of Christ leaves a mark. The Greek word for "mark" is stigma. It references a scar designating service or ownership. Claiming and following Jesus Christ as Savior and Lord is to acknowledge having been "bought with a price" (2 Corinthians 6:17) and having become the "purchased possession" of God (Ephesians 1:14). Far from disgrace or humiliation, our association with Jesus is one of humble gratitude, willing service, and close resemblance to Him. Peter and John preached Jesus to the antagonistic religious leaders, speaking with boldness and assurance even though facing brutal persecution. It was noted that they had "been with Jesus" (Acts 4:13).

Loving Father, help me exhibit Your mark today.

TRANSFORMATIONAL JOURNAL – DAY 15

How will I exhibit the cross of Christ in my life today?

_____

_____

_____

_____

_____

_____

_____

_____

_____

_____

፠)(፠

TRANSFORMATIONAL JOURNEY – DAY 16

Separate From the Evil Culture (Leviticus 18:3)

"According to the doings of the land of Egypt...you shall not do; and according to the doings of the land of Canaan, where I am bringing you, you shall not do." God explicitly instructed His people not to imitate the culture from which He freed them or the culture to where He was taking them. No matter where His people are, the distinct call is to holiness. "Come out from among them and be separate" (2 Corinthians 6:17). We are in this morally bankrupt world but are not to be influenced by it or its devolving standards. No matter the current-day expansion of moral boundaries, God never changes. He will never create any allowance that accommodates wicked behavior or sinful preferences.

Father, purify and separate me to Yourself.

TRANSFORMATIONAL JOURNAL – DAY 16

What worldly influence is restricting my reflection of Christ's likeness?

_____

_____

_____

_____

_____

_____

_____

_____

_____

୫ୠୠ

TRANSFORMATIONAL JOURNEY – DAY 17

Settling For Coins in the Gravel (Colossians 3:2, KJV)

"Set your affection on things above, not on things on the earth." While on a recent vacation in the mountains, I noticed three coins on the gravel driveway. For whatever reason, I found myself slowly pacing the driveway in search of more coins. There I was, surrounded by God's majestic beauty and tranquility, yet painstakingly walking back and forth, head down, looking for things of insignificant value. Too often, we spend precious time settling for the insignificant or counterfeit thrills and elusive fulfillment of this world while ignoring the abundant life and internal contentment God offers.

Oh, God, help me lift my eyes from the trivialities of this life and look to You, my Creator, Redeemer, and Source of strength, contentment, and abundance.

TRANSFORMATIONAL JOURNAL – DAY 17

What "trivial things" will I exchange for things of eternal significance?

_____

_____

_____

_____

_____

_____

_____

_____

_____

_____

TRANSFORMATIONAL JOURNEY – DAY 18

Reformation Is a Natural Outcome of Genuine Repentance (2 Chronicles 30-31:1)

Transformation occurs with two catalysts: repentance and reformation. After revival motivated repentance in the Israelites, King Hezekiah removed the pillars, images, altars, and high places of the false gods they previously worshiped. Repentance begins the inward change initiated by a penitent, submissive heart and the supernatural work of the Holy Spirit. However, along with this inner change, outer change is also necessary. Reformation involves changing sinful situations, environments, and habits in need of repentance. Transformation is difficult in an unchanged environment. Continuing sinful habits, relationships, and environments reveals a lack of wholehearted commitment to repentance and opens the door for reentry. There is no negotiation in genuine repentance.

Father, I surrender to Your transforming work. Please remove, repair, and restore as You desire.

TRANSFORMATIONAL JOURNAL – DAY 18

What is God removing, repairing, or restoring in my life today?

ॐ

TRANSFORMATIONAL JOURNEY – DAY 19

The Excellency of Christ (Philippians 3:8-9)

"...That I may gain Christ and be found in Him..." To gain Christ implies living to win or obtain His favor and fellowship. This does not suggest a works-based effort. Rather, it reveals an active engagement, fueled by intentional passion and determined pursuit of a deeper relationship with Him. It is the replacement of mere status quo with the fevered longing of more. Being found in Christ means anyone who knows us is not surprised by our association with Jesus or our intense pursuit of Him. Any inquiry into or observation of our lives confirms our identity in Him, and faithfulness to Him, until either He returns or He calls us home.

Father God, bind my heart to You until it beats in rhythm with Your own.

TRANSFORMATIONAL JOURNAL – DAY 19

What does my heart reveal about my intimacy and fellowship with God?

_____

_____

_____

_____

_____

_____

_____

_____

_____

_____

ॐ

TRANSFORMATIONAL JOURNEY – DAY 20

Others May; You May Not (Deuteronomy 18:14)

"As for you, the LORD your God has not appointed such for you." I recall my dad's usual reply to my childish requests to participate in some questionable, disruptive, or unsafe activity other children were enjoying. "Others may; you may not." God repeated this theme to the Israelites when warning against worshiping the pagan gods of the Canaanites. He knew the futility and danger of chasing useless idols. He also knows the same about the myriad idols we erect and prioritize over Him. Even comparing ourselves to others who tolerate a less spiritual lifestyle is foolish. God may be calling us to a closer walk—a deeper intimacy of holiness—with Him than others choose to follow.

Father, I choose to walk closer and pursue deeper intimacy with You.

TRANSFORMATIONAL JOURNAL – DAY 20

How is God drawing me into deeper intimacy with Him?

_____

_____

_____

_____

_____

_____

_____

_____

_____

ঙ৩৫৪

TRANSFORMATIONAL JOURNEY – DAY 21

The Absence of Bad Does Not Equal Good
(Ephesians 4:17-32)

I find myself frequently guilty of justifying what God wants to remove. Though I grasp the "not bad" and "there's nothing wrong with it," He continues refining and transforming me to make me more like Jesus (Romans 8:29). He stands before me, hands outstretched to receive the things holding me back and the specific desire to which I cling (Hebrews 12:1). He awaits all the traits and habits I am "putting off" to replace them with what I am to "put on" (Ephesians 4:20-23). Out with the old, in with the new (2 Corinthians 5:17). Just because there is nothing wrong with something does not make it God's best.

Father, help me let go and trust that You know what is best for me.

TRANSFORMATIONAL JOURNAL – DAY 21

What un-Christlike behavior, action, or mindset is resisting God's transforming work?

_____

_____

_____

_____

_____

_____

_____

_____

_____

_____

ॐ

TRANSFORMATIONAL JOURNEY – DAY 22

When God Takes Us Into New Places (Joshua 3:4)

"You have not passed this way before." As Joshua prepared the Israelites to enter the Promised Land, he gave specific instructions for this new venture. They were to wait until the Ark of the Covenant passed by. Then, they were to follow, but not too closely so they could see where it went. Finally, they were to purify themselves in preparation for the wonders God was about to perform. Should God move us into new places or seasons of life, may we wait until He leads. Let us not get impatient or impertinent, neither rushing ahead nor presuming we know the way.

Loving Father, may I carefully and specifically follow Your lead, while purifying myself—removing the dust from my past and renewing the commitment for Your future.

TRANSFORMATIONAL JOURNAL – DAY 22

Where and how is God leading me today?

_____

_____

_____

_____

_____

_____

_____

_____

_____

ॐ

TRANSFORMATIONAL JOURNEY – DAY 23

Becoming Just Like Jesus (Colossians 1:27)

"Christ in you, the hope of glory." The hope of the Christian faith is spending eternity with God. This hope is based solely on the forgiveness, regeneration, and righteousness obtained through Jesus Christ alone. Evidence of that hope is the Holy Spirit living within and influencing a person's lifestyle choices, behaviors, and mindset. While we are still earthbound, God's transformational process continues "until Christ is formed in you" (Galatians 4:19). He lovingly and relentlessly refines His followers to conform us to the image of His Son, Jesus Christ (Romans 8:29). He does this, not to manipulate or force us into being something we are not, nor ever can be on our own, but so we may stand before God the Father, complete in Christ Jesus (Colossians 1:28).

Father, please make me more like You.

TRANSFORMATIONAL JOURNAL – DAY 23

What is God asking of me today to make me more like Jesus?

_____

_____

_____

_____

_____

_____

_____

_____

_____

ॐﹾﻚﻩ

TRANSFORMATIONAL JOURNEY – DAY 24

God Makes the Distinction (Exodus 8:23)

"I will make a difference between My people and your people." When God brought the plagues against Egypt, He safeguarded the Israelites from the harm of judgment. This was a sign to Pharaoh of God's sovereign power and favor and also confirmation of His divine separation. God distinguishes between His people and those who are not. He differentiates between the holy and the unholy, the clean and unclean (Leviticus 10:10). He separates between those who obey Him wholeheartedly and those who give mere lip service (Matthew 15:8). There is coming a day of judgment when Christ will make the ultimate and eternal distinction between those who truly know Him and those who do not (Matthew 7:21-23).

Father God, help me accept and apply Your holy distinction in my life. May all I do glorify You and point others to You.

TRANSFORMATIONAL JOURNAL - DAY 24

How is God demonstrating His holy distinction in my life today?

_____

_____

_____

_____

_____

_____

_____

_____

_____

※)(₢

TRANSFORMATIONAL JOURNEY – DAY 25

When Hearts Desire Earthly Trinkets, Heaven's Treasure Remains Hidden (Matthew 6:19-20)

"Do not lay up for yourselves treasures on earth... but lay up for yourselves treasures in heaven." When we crave something secondary, it is difficult to want God's best. If our expectation is a 10-speed bike, it is hard to envision God's Maserati. By grasping our objects of affection, it is hard to pray, "Thy will, not mine, be done." Settling for the world's meager meal makes it hard to accept God's abundance. By saying, "Lift up your eyes," (John 4:35) Jesus urges, "Get a new vision; renew your expectations. Open your heart to what I have for you. Surrender your desires to Me. Let Me fulfill your longings. Only in Me will you find what you seek and truly need."

Father, may You be my heart's desire.

TRANSFORMATIONAL JOURNAL – DAY 25

What personal priority, preference, or value does God want to transform?

_____

_____

_____

_____

_____

_____

_____

_____

_____

৪০০৪

TRANSFORMATIONAL JOURNEY – DAY 26

God's Sovereign Control Over Everything (Ezekiel 14:23)

In the seemingly random chaos of life, it is easy to presume there is no intentional purpose or control— no sovereign orchestration. However, there are no surprises or "uh-oh" moments with God. He wastes no event, no matter how small and insignificant or global and cataclysmic. God says, "You shall know that I have done nothing without cause." So, when adversity strikes, when raging storms blow into our lives, a better question than, "Why is this happening?" might be, "God, what are You trying to teach me or do through this?" Although often painful, God's transformational process usually comes through changed environments.

Father God, You orchestrate all things. Help me trust Your heart, knowing You work all things for my overall good and Your ultimate glory.

TRANSFORMATIONAL JOURNAL – DAY 26

How is God sovereignly changing my lifestyle or environment(s)?

_____

_____

_____

_____

_____

_____

_____

_____

_____

_____

TRANSFORMATIONAL JOURNEY – DAY 27

Do People See Jesus When They Look At Me?
(Colossians 3:3)

My life is "hidden with Christ in God." In such a radical, transformed environment, may we live our lives so in love with God, so aligned with Him, so intimate with Him, that people see Jesus when they look at us. May we exhibit peace in our storms, grace in our conflicts, compassion for the hurting, forgiveness when wronged, commitment in service, and unconditional love for others. Let our lifestyles honor Him as we deny ourselves daily, take up our crosses, and follow Him. May we reflect His likeness as we submit daily to the Holy Spirit's influence.

Loving, Heavenly Father, when my days on earth are over and I enter Your presence, may all who reflect on my life be encouraged by my resemblance to You.

TRANSFORMATIONAL JOURNAL – DAY 27

How can I better reflect Christlikeness in all my interactions?

_____

_____

_____

_____

_____

_____

_____

_____

_____

༄༅

TRANSFORMATIONAL JOURNEY – DAY 28

Do You Want To Be Well? (Exodus 15:26)

"I am the LORD, who heals you." Heartache and soul wounds are part of the human experience. Everyone endures some form of adversity in his or her lifetime. Thankfully, God wants to heal our broken places. "He heals the brokenhearted and binds up their wounds" (Psalm 147:3). "The Lord is near to those who have a broken heart, and saves such as have a contrite spirit" (Psalm 34:18). But He usually does not heal what is not surrendered to Him. He asks us as He asked the sick man by the pool of Bethesda, "Do you *want* to be made well?" Wholeness involves personally surrendering our broken places to God and accepting His healing.

Father, help me surrender my specific pain-points and soul wounds to You in preparation for Your transformational healing.

TRANSFORMATIONAL JOURNAL – DAY 28

What pain-points or soul wounds am I willing to surrender to God?

_____

_____

_____

_____

_____

_____

_____

_____

_____

_____

꧁꧂

TRANSFORMATIONAL JOURNEY – DAY 29

Expectantly Await Christ's Return (2 Peter 3:10-12)

"But the ·day of the Lord will come as a thief in the night. Therefore...what manner of persons ought you to be in holy conduct and godliness, looking for and hastening the coming of the day of God?" Jesus warned His followers to pay close attention and be prepared for His return so it would not surprise us. "Watch therefore, and pray always" (Luke 21:34-36). The Lord's imminent return encourages living in a constant state of joyful anticipation and steadfast service. Our daily conduct and interactions should demonstrate a readiness and urgency to complete our missions, while allowing Him to transform us daily into His image. We do this so when we meet Him, we may stand complete in Him.

Father, I am surrendered to Your will and ready for Your return. Please complete Your work in me.

TRANSFORMATIONAL JOURNAL – DAY 29

How am I preparing for Christ's imminent return?

_____

_____

_____

_____

_____

_____

_____

_____

_____

TRANSFORMATIONAL JOURNEY – DAY 30

Satisfied to Awake in His Likeness (Psalm 17:15)

"I shall be satisfied when I awake in Your likeness." One day, those who have placed their faith in Jesus will awake in His likeness, not just His presence. In this life, though struggling with the process of transformation, we are bathed in His presence. But then, face to face (1 Corinthians 13:12), we will be like Him, for we will see Him as He is (1 John 3:2). Our transformation will be complete. We will fall asleep in the earthly dimension and awake in the heavenly.

Oh, glorious day, Father, to be with You and see You face to face! To be in Your likeness, no more to struggle, stumble, or fall in this body bound by unheavenly desires. That will be true satisfaction and blessedness evermore!

TRANSFORMATIONAL JOURNAL - DAY 30

How has this 30-day journey better prepared me for eternity?

_____

_____

_____

_____

_____

_____

_____

_____

_____

_____

ABOUT THE AUTHOR

A lifelong student of Scripture, Nate Stevens has also enjoyed a banking career in a variety of leadership roles. He is the author of *Matched 4 Life* and *Deck Time with Jesus* as well as a contributing author on several of the Moments Books (*Billy Graham Moments, Romantic Moments, Divine Moments, Spoken Moments, Christmas Moments, Stupid Moments,* etc.). He writes online articles for ChristianDevotions.us and KingdomWinds.com as well as several other ministries. Additionally, he co-founded and leads Fusion, a Christian singles ministry. A popular speaker and teacher at conferences, seminars and Bible study groups, he speaks on a wide variety of topics. Nate has two adult children. He and his wife, Karen, live near Charlotte, North Carolina.

Follow Nate and find more resources at:

www.natestevens.net.

Made in the USA
Columbia, SC
17 September 2020

19530428R00041